# Something Will Change Me

poems of soul
and spirit
**Don Hynes**

Something Will Change Me
Copyright © 2024 by Don Hynes.

All rights reserved. No part of this book may be used or reproduced in any manner whatsoever without written permission of the publisher except in the case of brief quotations embodied in critical articles or reviews.

Library of Congress Cataloging In Publication Data
Names: Hynes, Don—author
Title: Something Will Change Me: Poems of Soul and Spirit
Description: Portland, Oregon : Slender Arrow Press
Identifiers: LCCN — 2024910420

ISBN — 978-0-9741648-6-1 (paperback)
ISBN — 978-0-9741648-8-5 (ebook)

For more information contact:
Slender Arrow Press
429 NE 29th Ave.
Portland OR 97232

Editing by Sandy Brown Jensen
Photography by Ann B. Foorman, Don Hynes, Sandy Brown Jensen, and Louis MacKenzie

Cover photo by Sandy Brown Jensen
Cover and interior design by Abbey Gregory
https://abbeygregory.com

Contact Don Hynes:
info@donhynes.com
https://donhynes.com

# Praise for *Something Will Change Me*

"Don embeds soul-inspired meaning and healing spells in and between every word, the harvest of a life deeply lived. Time stands still as I read ... I am renewed. Pure magic!"

- Will T Wilkinson, #1 *Wall Street Journal* best-selling author

"This collection of deeply imaginative poems will, I am certain, change you. You need only read patiently and with love. They are a gift to us all."

- Louis MacKenzie, Professor Emeritus, University of Notre Dame

"Having followed Don's poetry for years, it is wonderful to have these selected poems to reinvigorate the heart and open more fully to the dimensions of the inner world as reflected through the dynamics of nature. These poems will let you sip deeply into the mystery of your life."

- David Kyle, PhD author and teacher

"Don knows what he loves: the night, the Mystery, grace, in-between places, the oldest trees and islands and how to tell a secret—all things I love, too, and I love the way he remembers them back to me in these poems."

- Sandy Brown Jensen, author, photographer,

# Contents

| | |
|---|---|
| Author's Preface | XV |
| Introduction | XIX |

**Spirit Walk**

| | |
|---|---|
| New Story | 3 |
| Leaving No Trace | 4 |
| Night World | 5 |
| Solstice | 6 |
| World Almost New | 7 |

**Across the Great Distance**

| | |
|---|---|
| Fullness of Desire | 11 |
| Thawing the Hardness | 12 |
| Daring to Raise My Eyes | 13 |
| Across the Great Distance | 14 |
| The Lion Waits | 15 |
| Breathe in Water | 16 |

**The Sharpened Point of Love**

| | |
|---|---|
| Spoken from Silence | 21 |
| Knowledge of a Seed | 22 |
| Mystery of Owl | 23 |
| Dream Whale | 24 |
| Soundless Yes | 25 |
| Something New | 26 |
| Sound of Life | 27 |

Asleep in the Body of Salmon
    Rare and Precious    31
    Root Cellar    32
    Child of My Age    33
    Asleep in the Body of Salmon    34
    Creation Song    35
    Years of Silence    36
    Before Descent    37

To Love What is Close
    Impossible Beauty    41
    Like Rivers We Pour    42
    On the Centennial    43
    To Love What is Close    44
    Waiting in the Shadows    45
    Ancient Son    46
    Dream of Night    47
    Speaking in Tongues    48

Words of Belonging
    Moon of Our Gravitation    53
    Plum Tree    54
    Their World    55
    Return to the Forest    56
    Endless Page    57
    First Light    58
    Finding My Birth    59
    Circle of Two    60

Hall of Dragons
- Quieting the Noise — 65
- Bird Nest — 66
- Order of the Golden Ball — 67
- Guarding the Door — 68
- Something Will Change Me — 69
- Suffer the Night — 70
- Welcome the Unfinished — 71
- Choose Each Day — 72

Holding Her Sorrow
- Laid to Rest — 77
- Winter Path — 78
- On the Bridge — 79
- How It Will Be — 80
- Say the Goodbye — 81
- Time Bound Links — 82
- Preparing Witness — 83
- Walks in Moonlight — 84
- Unwrapping the Message — 85
- Bear Knows — 86
- Headlights — 87

Melody of the Stranger
- Song of Winter — 91
- Placing My Prayer — 92
- Melody of the Stranger — 93
- River Story — 94
- Language of Light — 95
- Under the Miller's Wheel — 96

Melody of the Stranger *(ctd.)*
   Who Will Find Me   97
   Sound of Breathing   98
   Between Dreams   99
   Song Line   100
   Fisher of the Dark   101

Strengthened in Darkness
   Grandmother's Blanket   105
   Across the Alvord   106
   Unfasten the Lock   107
   After a Night of Rain   108
   Earth Walk   109
   Room at Last   110
   Full of Grace   111

Drop the Skin Face
   Time to Live   115
   Grace to Her Becoming   116
   Washboard Road   117
   Surrendered to Awakening   118
   Campground of His Ancient Home   119
   Soul Kitchen   120
   Janitor in the House of Soul   121
   An Old Tree Falls   122
   Drop the Skin Face   123

## Voicing the Incantation

| | |
|---|---|
| Rope of Stillness | 127 |
| Voicing the Incantation | 128 |
| Rushing Tide | 129 |
| Prepare for the Mountain | 130 |
| Written Across the Sky | 131 |
| Tear Another Page | 132 |
| Instead She Flowers | 133 |

## Where the River Goes

| | |
|---|---|
| For I Am Water | 137 |
| Dark Green Solitude | 138 |
| Where Bones Grind | 139 |
| In the Hour Before Dawn | 140 |
| Before the Sky Grows Dark | 141 |
| Choirs of Knowing | 142 |
| Words of the Disciple | 143 |
| Dark Heaven | 144 |
| Then We Will Not Speak | 145 |

Also by Don Hynes

*Slender Arrow*
*Out From Under*
*The Living Dark*
*The Irish Girl*

# Something Will Change Me

Author's Preface

# Author's Preface

The sound of wind in tall firs and the rhythmic crash of waves became my companions. I knelt as pilgrim beside the fullness of tides, the rush of forest rivers, cupping my hands to capture their murmurs. Years of such listening are woven in these poems.

You'll find the beauty of the San Juan Islands, the fathomless waters of the Salish sea, and the grit of Portland streets. There's a celebration of love's embrace, and a raw honesty as time, wind and water reveal the face beneath the mask.

Perhaps within this collection, you'll glimpse a reflection of your own journey, a guide to continue. If so, I'm honored to share these poems with you.

Don Hynes
April 2024

Introduction

# Introduction

The poetry of Don Hynes is rich and clear, moves and speaks gently, never calling attention to itself as performance. Yet there is something monumental here, in the overarching thread of the interplay between the inner and outer landscapes.

Central to this ecology are the ideas of vision and voice. Don takes the time to look and listen to the world around him and gives voice to that world. The natural objects of his gaze - trees, roots, water, animals – are liberated under his pen.

A striking example of this appears in a poem titled "Olive Tree." In it, Hynes peels away the outer shell of the tree. He invites the reader to envisage a dulcimer within the wood. Inside the instrument a song awaits; inside the song a dance, inside the dance he finds God, evoked in the rhythmic breath of a song.

The title of Don's current collection, Something Will Change Me, is more complex than it seems. The "something" can express both certainty and the indefinite. "Something," the agent of change, but not yet definable. A similar richness is introduced in "will." Is it a simple future tense or an assertion of that which has already been determined, remembered, or created?

The chapter headings act as an itinerary, a witness to the change expressed in Don's years of poetry. The titles tell their own story, and like the poems themselves, they can be seen as stylized, reconstructed, or imagined versions of something not wholly defined. Such is the adventure, the joy, and the discovery of reading these poems.

Appearing first, "Spirit Walk" invites the reader back to something original when the spirit, formless and essential, sets itself in motion. Is it already looking for that "something" that will transform it, will give it form? As it moves, it encounters the "Sharpened Point of Love," which simultaneously suggests pleasure, seductiveness, threat, and danger.

Next comes the chapter "Asleep in the Body of Salmon." This title references the "jagged teeth and furious jaw" of the salmon as well as the "wild desire" of the woman asleep inside it. This gives further definition to the "sharpened point of love."

Despite the allure of wildness, the spirit traveler in the poem "To Love What is Close," may have found enough to stop the journey (" I don't think I'm going"). Resting, he finds "Words of Belonging," which may suggest on the one hand, the ideas of sharing, togetherness, and communion; on the other, the notion of words themselves—the very DNA of poetry. The next chapter heading, "Hall of Dragons" introduces the exotic and at times frightening nature of relationships.

As a complement to this comes the tenderness of "Holding Her Sorrow" and the "Melody of the Stranger." These suggest the awareness and cherishing of the partner's otherness. Their embrace and communion speak of love "Strengthened in Darkness."

That strength gives the narrator the courage to "Drop the Skin Face," to abandon the surface and the posing to assume something more natural, even wild. In so doing, we readers are taken to a place where "Voicing the Incantation" is not only possible, but necessary.

The incantation is both the song and the conjuring of the mystical, the world of the spirit, the spirit of the world, and yes, the "Spirit Walk." It is "Where the River Goes"; and where it has gone is this very collection of magical poems that will, I am certain, change you. You need only read patiently and with love. They are Don's gift to us all.

Louis MacKenzie<br>
Professor Emeritus of French<br>
University of Notre Dame

Spirit Walk

# New Story

What will rise and what will follow,
what will fall into the yawning deep?
In the earth the sound of water
and rush of stones.

It is the time of the ancient
and the time of soil.
Veins open with silver
and the round moon shines
luminescent gold.

Great fish break surface,
grasslands thrum with becoming.
Broken bones dissolve into wheat,
people gather to the heartbeat of drums.

Out of the east a bright light comes walking
and up from the sea diamonds emerge.
Remembered and forgotten
the great book closes

and the whole earth opens
to the new story,
ready and waiting
for that story to be told.

## Leaving No Trace

Birds flock on the tide
while dark clouds of rain drive onshore,
clearing skies over the island.
Gracefully, they circle and land,
circle and land, gathering.

I sit quietly, sipping
on the early hours
of soft light and shadow.
The silent earth, teaching
deep root and letting go,
lightens my footsteps

until like the ancients
I leave no trace
but the imprint of kindness
left on the souls
I've dared to love.

# Night World

By day the light upon water
is brilliant and bright,
securing the outlines
of what is safe and real.

By night, now shimmering,
the moon invites you deeper;
everything trembles in this light,
speaking through shadows.

If I had the courage,
I'd live in night wonder,
walking forest paths
with slivers of silver
breaking through the trees,

at peace in the stillness,
awake from my dreams.

# Solstice

Rain cleanses the morning
with clouds from the Pacific
riding the vast arc of ocean wind,
falling upon the earth
to the root of our faith,
soaking deep the dark womb
of renewal.

# World Almost New

When the storm passed,
light awakened the coastline
gray and shrouded,
sharp with detail.

The cabins, the old dock,
even the gulls in flight,
bathed in a world almost new;
as if sorrow were over
and we could begin again.

Across the Great Distance

# Fullness of Desire

To learn, the earth takes
a slow, steady ponder, listening
to the sounds and silences,
especially the silences,
paying homage with attention
until something dark and unseen
breaks into awareness,
bursting like a mushroom
with the full throat of desire.

# Thawing the Hardness

Ice forms at night,
and the old fear rises,
memory of dark and bitter cold,
feeling not death but survival,

and all we did to stay alive
when life was only suffering;
men and women like iron,
the only sound wind and bitter voices.

Dawn spreads now from the east
come to replace the shadows,
thawing with a breath of new light
the kindness fear obscures;
the gift that saw us through.

# Daring to Raise My Eyes

I reach out
over the horizon,
cracked and weakened
by struggle and death
and all that's fallen.

Daring to raise my eyes,
I call out, a bird-like sound,
giving myself to this day,
abandoning desire
for all except you.

# Across the Great Distance

Winds gust from the south
pushing the flood tide
into gravel reaches,
soaking the stone feet
of an ancient rock wall
with images carved
by all that's gone before.

Vigilant in what is yet to come,
and from this place between
past runes and future dreams,
I call to you, joining us
across the great distance.

# The Lion Waits

The lion in me waits,
hungry for unseen light,
gnawing on a hollow bone
to gather strength
from the river
beneath the Earth.

## Breathe in Water

I sit within the arc of aging
strong with the weight
of years in silence,
worn round as rock
against the tide.

The tides of gain and loss
shape and reshape the world,
while below brilliant star fish
breathe in water,
turning salt and sea
to light.

The Sharpened Point of Love

# Spoken from Silence

Stark white paper and midnight ink,
sunlit pale-yellow plaster,
big drop rain flowing rivulets in the street
and your hair swirling in curves of fine silver.

Against the tide of violence
something spoken from the silence
like an arrow parting air
with the sharpened point of love.

# Knowledge of a Seed

High in the gray sky
tall firs sway in a wind
not felt beside the pond,
abandoned by geese and ducks
even in this mild winter.

I plod along the empty path,
and watch branches above
wave in somber colors,
as I wave to the lives I've lived,
gone like the geese of winter.

I wonder what will come on this wind,
if I will rise like evergreen sap
for another spring, another pulse of life,
while I search through inner darkness
for the knowledge of a seed,
and the spark of love to see it through.

# Mystery of Owl

Part of me enjoys
the dark, wet tangle
that will not rise
nor come in from the night,
where the mystery of owl
speaks to the sea,
wings spread in darkness.

# Dream Whale

I pick my way beneath
the oily wooden dock,
pilings down in sea water,
invisible in the dark,
and I feel the old fear.

I raise and lower my feet in gravelly sand,
edging between barnacle-covered posts
then out on a rotted step
where I hear a great exhale.

In the wide cove a whale,
silver and magnificent,
arches her massive fluke,
calling me out to sea.

# Soundless Yes

Here in this room,
this morning,
no machine sound,
no gears or clockwork
falling into place,
just the soundless yes
of your hair upon the pillow,
your breath soft in pre-dawn light.

## Something New

Everything continues as it has
until it doesn't,
water flows downhill
until it won't,
dinosaurs sleep in ice
with green grass in their teeth,
fearless armies march
to Napoleon's last ditch.

Then the long pause
while power gathers
within the sleeping earth,
giants awaken and stars come to life
with songs of something new.

# Sound of Life

There's light on the headboard
from a break in the curtains
and the sound of you stirring.
Despite the list of tasks,
and the burdens carried,
the curtain is open,
just a fraction, but open
to the sunlight
and the sound of life
from your sleeping body.

Asleep in the Body of Salmon

# Rare and Precious *(for Linda)*

She's a gift, you see,
rare and precious
as wild grass
or heron in flight;
unpredictable,
beyond imitation,
gemstone perfect.

I swear off disbelief
while she dresses,
the fullness of life
so unexpected,

and I practice like a child
on the impossible violin,
amazed and delighted
over and again
by the appearance
of her music.

## Root Cellar

Gunnysacks cover the winter crop,
the root cellar dry and warm in its burrow;
outside the sea lifts in the driving wind,
the long arc of sand shaped and reshaped
by the fierce hand that forms the air
and lifts the gulls in one motion.

Part of me wants to lay down
in the dust of potatoes,
the ripening odor of apples,
to sleep and wake
with the dreams of bear
and hunger of a newborn.

I want to fall further than night
into the color behind stars,
the deep dark of space beyond all light
and let long months go by
with hard-shelled squash and seed corn,
while I nurture and dry my desire.

Then like an Irish spud
send out long, thin eyes
for the first sight of tomorrow.

# Child of My Age

Sun is down in its winter home,
barely visible above naked branches,
the valley without rain
for the first time in weeks.
Dry and bright, the day opens
and I meet it, worn places
flaking off like decayed skin,
and beneath the roughage
something pink and new.

A baby born from an old man
like the miracle of Abraham,
child of my age coming forth
with words fully formed,
yearning for the milk of life
and bright green forest,
still wailing with hunger
after all these years.

## Asleep in the Body of Salmon

There's a woman asleep
in the body of salmon
behind the jagged teeth
and furious jaw,
parting the river
with wild desire.

# Creation Song

    Driving through the rough-hewn gate
    past the carved wooden sign
    and down the gravel lane,
    I found the broad russet hay field
    lifted into autumn maple
    or perhaps rising up
    to greet me like an old friend.

    Every tree and trembling fern
    had a voice in the slanted sunlight,
    the rubbed bronze earth
    reaching out with a song.

# Years of Silence

We get used to winter's gray lid
when sunlight becomes a memory,
color fading into the mash of leaves
on wet streets and sidewalks,
the ceiling of our expectations
coming down like rain.

Standing still we're old growth trees,
catching mist in our moss covered branches,
roots shot through with years of silence,
falling into winter's sleep
to grow the many songs of spring.

# Before Descent

The sun is south
in the morning sky
as if it were leaving us
with colorless farewell;
the gold of autumn burned
to brilliant white.

With bare arms
and empty branches,
the hunger of the earth
outlines the darkness
before descent,
and the long rest
of winter.

To Love What is Close

# Impossible Beauty

The color green
in morning light,
black wings
against blue sky,
leaves burned gold
with the shock
of a photograph.

Her body rises
through concrete,
speaks in wind
and cloud,
her dreams and loss,
the impossible beauty
of a bird.

# Like Rivers We Pour

The tiniest parts of us
are what appear,
stuff you can see
like clouds off the ocean
and big drop rain.

We open like mountains,
dive in cold water,
yet this spark of light
we give a name
is but a glimmer,
like snow melt
and passing leaves.

We show our faces
then are gone,
and like rivers we pour.

# On the Centennial *(for William)*

You spent your life writing poems
shaped from the earth
with the quiet force of water,
reminding us of the danger
putting anyone on a pedestal.
Now that you're gone
we dress you up in hero's cloth,

but I recall the dry dust
of the internment camps,
the forgotten people
on the edge of town,
the hubris of war
and the darkness that waits
beyond the frail light
of our traveling circus.

I remember these things, Bill,
and won't forge them
into a statue.

# To Love What is Close

I found this place
before winter snows,
green and tender
with the wet smell of life.

Resting here with wounds healing,
the impulse to go on
quieted by the river,
limbs like drooping cedars
let go and touch the earth.

Though the pass ice is melting,
the way across the mountains
opening for spring,
I don't think I'm going.

The smell of apples
and litter of oaks
is enough of what I want,
nurturing the urge
to love what is close.

# Waiting in the Shadows *(for Louis)*

    Poetry is a private affair
    born from the unlit
    in the embrace of silence;
    no one around to watch,
    just me and a few words
    waiting in the shadows,
    loitering in the dark
    like hungry lovers.

# Ancient Son

Dense as stone,
stubborn as thorn,
something within him
aligns with the stars,
finds solace in the tide.

Infinite and weightless,
blood dark from suffering,
my proud boy
looks into the dawn
with the fearless gaze
of an ancient son.

# Dream of Night

The world stirred
with water flowing
through the ebb tide,
low sun slanting
on the morning sea,
gulls circling the rocks
crying, come awake!

As the dream of night
hatched like a perfect egg,
we opened our eyes
into the very first light.

# Speaking in Tongues

The old man's shell cracks
thick as a tombstone,
hard as walnut,
hungry for the green wave.

With tears of desire
his white arms reach,
uncoiling, irresistible,
speaking in tongues,
searching for God.

Words of Belonging

# Moon of Our Gravitation

You raise your cup
assured I will receive it.
This gesture says it all,
how we are together
with no need to tear down,
to feed the beast of not belonging.

Some days the tide runs strong,
highs and lows much greater.
They say it is the moon
and I wonder about swirling water
and the desire that pulls it toward the sea.

As the tide runs swift, perhaps
we too can be without restraint,
the moon of our gravitation
the touch of your hand
on a teacup.

## Plum Tree

No one told the plum tree
about the end of the world,
or the fat layered seal
about oceans passing.

Changes come,
but a pup still cries
and salmon rush strong
when the last of the snow
melts down to the sea.

I tell myself of a far reach
where her truth pours down
like veins from the mountain.
We should stop
before time runs out,

and let the river
tell us once more
about the old way,
the ancient streams
of thought and feeling,

as the plum tree opens
when the sun is hot
and the soft red fruit
slowly ripens.

# Their World

We'll talk sometime
but not now,
not for a while,
maybe in the next life
or when the sun
lights the river
and rocks shine.

Maybe when the earth
gives back what we left
when we thought
we had so much,
yet all we had
was water in our hands
and the smell of green -
intoxicating, delirious.

Down the narrow trail
to the sound of sea lions
barking their belonging,
we wandered into their world,
the one we thought was ours.

# Return to the Forest

I am the face behind the face,
the watcher behind eyes.
I'll slip this skin
like a bright fish
glistening in the sun,
wriggling free of your hands
back into the deep pool,
a glint of gold and silver
darting through the stream.

That color, that liquid,
the shining skin, that is me
but not all of me;
I am what the river cannot hold.
I swim inside this skin,
but I'll slip it soon
and take another.

The stars will take me
and warm sand
waiting at the shore.
The deep sea will take me
and trails along the mountain.

Where I go you will not follow,
yet I'll break from the brush
to see you once more,
a deer with her fawns
crossing the road
thin-legged and lithe.

# Endless Page

The words I speak or write,
do they really matter
beneath the waterfall of life,
all the tragedy and loss
and wandering in the dark?
I have so much fear
I don't acknowledge,
so much I hoped for,
wanting the world
to answer my longing.

When I listen
I hear the old voice
within the roar,
a plodding slow-paced
reminder of the ancient,
spoken through sand
and broken monuments.

The rise and fall
and dreams of glory
like fallen leaves
and moldering earth,
a filament reaching
back through time,
threading me
into the weave
of all who've lived
and left a mark
on the endless page.

# First Light

I caught first light
in those few hours
when the innocence
of the world
played open
like a child's skirts,
twirling in the breeze
with the joy
of being alive.

# Finding My Birth

Something or someone calls
not from the dream time
but below the sea
where the sleek seal dives,
or in the belly of the rock
that gives shape to water,
or the land itself wanting to rise
through dry waving grass
and release on the wind.

Perhaps it's just me
struggling each day
to find my birth,
coming into the world
again and again
with a soul, a spirit
and such a frail body.

Weak before the forces
of time and knowledge,
broken like a twig
in the hands of the earth,
yet returning each morning
to the altar of the sacred.

I sing with the only voice I have
the words of belonging,
sung to the sea,
passing like a cloud.

# Circle of Two

We live within a circle of two,
not straying beyond our home
for a night and a day and another night;
the intimacy of life enough to feed us,
the food of our camp what we've gathered
from the clearing of our hearts.

Holding to each other
beneath the arc of sun and stars,
in the rooted soil where we are joined,
we burn back the pressing dark
with the fire we've tended,
alone together beside the river,
quiet as the trees.

Hall of Dragons

# Quieting the Noise

Singular and aware
I go within
to the place of silence,
dropping like a seal
into cold dark water.

# Bird Nest

In a nest inside my heart
a tiny bird lives,
peeping out to the world,
ready to fly into the unmarked sky.

Who I'll be when the bird leaves
is the writing of a poem,
words left beside the sea
tasting of salt,
touched by the wind.

# Order of the Golden Ball

In their last great meeting, medicine chiefs
rode down from the mountains,
bears crossed the wide rivers,
eagles left the coastline, beavers their dams,
trees pulled up roots, birds took wing,
whales swam upriver
and salmon walked the shore.

From the furthest horizon
Incas, Aztecs, ageless monks,
Sisters of the Silence,
and the Order of the Golden Ball
gathered with the ants and honeybees
and animals of every description.

When the ocean spoke,
her words inscribed a spread of clouds
before dissolving in the light
of a never seen star.

Then a groan from the earth
closed the ancient book
with the last gasp of compassion,
and the land opened in blood and ecstasy
as a new babe wailed with a cry of delight.

# Guarding the Door

A big city crow
sagged the power line,
giving me a one-eyed stare
of dark caution.

I saw a few birds,
dogs on leash,
but nothing else
spoke from the wild.

At the party
there were chances
to stumble and fall,
letting the wine talk
instead of my better angel,

but the outline of crow
guarded the door,
demanding silence.
How could I refuse?

# Something Will Change Me

I'll grow a beard,
live on the tide,
turn to stone
or dandelion,
then become water;

race in the ebb,
grow talons, take flight,
lay down as grass
sun brown and blazing.

Something will change me
yet behind the faces
I'll be the one watching,
rock shore deep,
hummingbird fast
back to the invisible.

## Suffer the Night

The cauldron comes to boil
laden with wounded flesh
and broken bones.
Witches mind the iron kettle,
while grim ogres without repentance
circle the fire with hungry eyes.

What was done to the least of these
rises in the lurid stew,
while the air fills with the dark smoke
of what might have been.

Encamped in the shadows,
beyond the flames and cries of the unforgiving,
two lonely angels camp in darkness,
keeping watch on the infernal.
The hour of sacrifice draws near;
there must be witness.

The fires will burn out, they always have.
When dawn comes upon the encampment
of blackened ash and ill-cast dreams,
another voice will speak the dream of the future.

Animals will gather as to a running stream,
wilderness will return bright and untarnished.
Suffer this night and welcome the day,
for this is the time of revelation.

# Welcome the Unfinished

The pause between night and day
suffers the wind, the rain,
the dark uncertainty,
to welcome the unfinished
with the grace of a bird.

Each day I go to this altar,
emptying the night
bucket after bucket,
until I've space enough
for the morning.

# Choose Each Day

I won't be nourished
by the glittering parade
of the soon-to-be-forgotten.

Rivers run white
in the first storms of November,
mountains ring with the sound
of water rushing to the sea.

Let me go down with leaves,
choose the submersion of rock
in the autumn flood.

Let me rise in darkness,
be fed by morning silence
and choose each day to say yes.

Holding Her Sorrow

# Laid to Rest

Thick moss covers the wet ground,
lifted beneath his hands
an opening for the burial.
He had come to this space
beside the cold flowing creek
to bring what was left of their memory;
he'd carried the corpse long enough.
Wildness called him from the dark
as he trekked to his old campsite.

Lifting back the green shroud
he pared away the soft earth,
placing a broken twig bundle
tied with dried flowers.
Arranging them to settle
in their resting place,
he folded the blanket of moss
over the grave in forest silence,
scooped dirt into the cut edges
until the wound was filled.

Then he tamped the earth
and turned back to the creek,
the frigid crossing and mended life
that was his own.

## Winter Path

Beneath the earth,
strength gathers dark
in stone lined caves,
not the time of rising but of rest.

Ice can break the oldest trees
but within their roots
the force of spring waits.

Go down with the rivers,
the deep peace of evergreen,
and let the well of darkness fill.

What must come will find its way
as we follow the winter path.

# On the Bridge

Along the border of night and day
old ghosts walk the valley
among the shades of beaver,
fox, raven and wolf,
their wisdom a voice within
to guide us through this dark.

Nothing can replace the wild,
but where dreams awake,
we take our place beside the fearless,
on the bridge of all that's past
to what may yet be born.

# How It Will Be

When lights go down,
and the wheels stop turning
we'll be left with night, morning quiet,
and the emptiness that welcomes.

We'll stop grinding our lives like corn
and circle dance with whales.
Our feet will drum the earth,
the rivers rise with joy,

and we'll be humans
beneath a star filled sky.

# Say the Goodbye

Wind drives up from the south
against the ebbing tide,
the surface chalked with waves.
I look out from the cabin
until the hour comes
to leave for the dock.

Time for another goodbye,
constant as the rain
and about as welcome.
I seem to empty again and again,
and wonder when joy will have its season.

The wind might lift me off this rock,
carry me to the ocean beyond.
I could get lost in water
and swim among whales

but for this morning
I'll just head down
to the long wooden pier
and say the goodbye.

# Time Bound Links

Along a mountain trail
beside the Clackamas,
buried in wooded beaches
rimming the Columbia,
lying in high dunes
between Sand Lake and the Pacific
you left fragments of your soul
remaining in time.

I find the shards
embedded in earth.
Picking them up,
desiccated and brittle,
I recall the days of their making;
weightless, I lift them to the sky,
blow my breath over the fragments
and they're gone, airborne,
returned to the timeless.

No gravestone or marker,
no imprint of the sacred,
just time bound links
in the long chain of life.

# Preparing Witness

He turns to rise with the sun
at the far edge of the world,
no temple or towering buddha,
just the lonely sound of garbage trucks
and smoke choked skies,
preparing witness
for what will come.

# Walks in Moonlight

Ripe and full the harvest moon rises
casting tree shadows from their tops
lifted to the star wheel.
No loneliness or garish glare,
just silver glow and silence.

Orion in the east
signals winter coming
yet still there is warmth
and the sweetness of corn.

The winds will pick up
bringing early storms,
rain again to soak the land,
but for now I walk in moonlight,
drinking deep the night.

# Unwrapping the Message

There's another message
the earth holds for you
when you're ready to unwrap it.

It tells of a kit fox, an old stag elk,
a river falling white and cold,
and within her, a place for you.

She's known all this time
you weren't broken;
spoken softly
that you might listen.

# Bear Knows

On the longest night of the year
I'm out of step like bear,
devoted to dark
and the quiet of snow.

Iris and daffodil
would have no color
except for waves of rain.

Hunger eats last summer's fat
while bear and I sleep, letting time
have its slow, darkening way.

# Headlights

Along the dark wet avenue,
you ply your way with other pilgrims,
radio on the morning news.

I reach out from this window,
the small rectangle you won't notice
as you pass a thousand others
in brick and wood.

Through thin glass I see you,
know a portion of your sorrow,
even your joy. I wish you life
my unknown friend.

May your headlights guide you
to something like the place
we once called home.

Melody of the Stranger

# Song of Winter

Rains and settling dark
softly soak the city.

In the mountains
forests rest white
and undisturbed.

Snow laden trees,
streets washed clean,
the timeless hymnal
open to the sky

in the deep throated
song of winter.

# Placing My Prayer

The moon rises
before the city wakes,
her bowl turned up
wanting to be filled.

Raccoons roam the streets,
deer browse the river,
the green world silent
beneath sheets of pavement,

as I place my prayers
on the altar of darkness.

# Melody of the Stranger

Just this morning,
with the sky full of rain,
I turn to the edge of light
in the far distance.

Cranky as a crow
I open like a spring bulb,
and go where I have not gone
for many years -
to the rim of a canyon,
the edge of a waterfall,

where the earth sings out
in the sweet-toned melody
of the stranger
I once knew as joy.

# River Story

From a cleft in sharp rock
water emerges from the mountain
to shine on lichen and a small stream
where swifts and marmots drink.

Gathering strength and falling,
brown rocks glisten, birds gather,
fish appear in circling eddies.
One stream reaches into another,
merging in deep ravines,
to fall out over stone ledges
alive with sunlight and oxygen.

River bears the weight,
rolling stones along the bottom,
feeding fish on their path home,
with herons tall and brooding along the banks.
Hawks circle above the broad stripe of water,
the grasslands alive with rich loam,

out onto the broad reach
where the bar breaks the sea
in one undaunted wave,
with stories of mountain,
crow and coyote, and the ocean
ravenous for all the river will tell.

# Language of Light

The tenderness of a soft breeze
dapples the morning sea
across the broad channel.

Seals break surface in their forage,
dolphins show black fins
in rolling breaths,
stirring the silence.

On the wind, the water,
the trembling earth,
a new-day testament begins again,
written without words
in the language of light.

# Under the Miller's Wheel

Who was I fooling?
The earth broke me,
ground me like winter wheat
for the coarsest bread.

"Grind some more,"
I said with bravado
and the earth was glad to oblige,
to pass me under the miller's wheel
until fine-sifted flour.

"Now make me food for all that lives."
And again the earth was glad
to bake me in her oven
and serve me to the people.

Buttered and brown
I passed through many hands
until a sad-eyed child
received a crumb,

and put to his mouth,
then I was whole.

# Who Will Find Me

Who will find me
hidden away in the warmth
of this dark cave?
Dreams to be dreamt,
visions to be honored,
the slow eating of fat
and the quiet heartbeat.

When the first salmon toil
over rock bedded streams,
when snow falls from the full
laden branches of evergreen,
when sun finds its way
along the great arc north,
then I will stretch and uncurl
from this lightless comfort,
and sing once more my hunger.

# Sound of Breathing

    I drop below to the peace
    beneath the city,
    under the basements,
    the pipes and channels,
    down where roots
    reach the sound
    of the old earth breathing.

# Between Dreams

Let it be dark,
this cave of contemplation.
No light need enter,
no warmth,
as winds howl
with the distant noise
of breaking ice
and cold shot trees.

Having given up the sun
and taken to the cavern,
I say what stone says,
the weight I've carried
laid down in darkness.

I breathe slowly
between dreams
with heart at rest
in the slow beat
of the earth.

# Song Line

Down the river canyon
water flows on and on,
from mountain lake
through desert rifts
of lava and ponderosa pine.

Beside the rapids
I hear the music,
the sound of water
over glistening rock,
holding the magic
of time unbroken.

Out of that cradle
the new earth is born,
down through the ages
again and again,
creating a song line
older than stone,
fresh as the morning.

# Fisher of the Dark

I throw a line into the dark,
the only bait hunger
and a sense of what waits
in the last hours of night.

There are tugs on the line,
then a bite, a face
from the dreamtime,
something to satisfy
my soul's craving.

I pull you in,
remembering how
we fought and danced
in the time we were given.

I passed you in a doorway,
glad to be unrecognized,
felt you behind me
in a crowded room,
but this dark morning
there's no escape.

I look and hold
your pulsing body,
and let there be
this knowing between us
before releasing you
back to the eternal.

Strengthened in Darkness

# Grandmother's Blanket

Crow came by
bringing news of the forest,
of salmon asleep in branch water,
beaver at work in the creek flows
and rooted beneath the ancient trees
the peace of earth gathered in pools
still and deep beyond measure.

Beside the old well
grandmother spreads her blanket,
her shells and stones laid out
in circular patterns,
her hands weaving stories
of what has been and what will be.

Crow carries us her heartbeat,
his black eyes and feathers
shaped by her in the long ago,
with a message to remember,
to not let our spirits be broken
as we follow the river.

## Across the Alvord

We scurry around
staying busy while winter
passes over the valley
and caps the mountains.
Warm air invites crows
to mass beside the river,
street people to flourish
in makeshift tents.

The rain lets up
and no one complains
except a few old-timers,
who remember snow
and the way of the Columbia.
They talk of beaver and wolf,
rivers filling the Coastal Range,
and along the foothills of the Cascades
floods that bore silt from glaciers.

They bag groceries,
pump gas for Costco
then with a grubstake
leave for the Idaho
and the mountains of Nevada.
We won't see them
until the snow gods return,
when people tire of hot air
and pray once more for winter.

# Unfasten the Lock

I see your struggle,
the weight etched
on your face
as you bear up
under the gravity
known only to you.

The world pulls down
while you strive
to gain altitude,
clawing at the trap
set on the day
you were born.

Don't bother
with confession,
just reach down
to the glint of metal
at the bottom of your soul,

the remembrance
of who you are
clear and shining,
and with that key
unfasten the lock.

# After a Night of Rain

After a night of rain
with clouds so dense
the moon barely shown,
a gray morning
of dim light and showers.

Evergreens stretch their limbs,
birds circle in the mist, and quietly
the plum tree flowers.

# Earth Walk

As birds wing over water
our souls travel this world
with tiny hearts beating,
fervent through
the rush of air.

Propelled from within
through suffering
and mortal ache,
life hollows
our urgent hunger

until reed-like
we give voice
to the music
of our earth walk.

# Room at Last

    Peering into the day
    there is the sea
    with tide and wind,
    the sound of birds
    and cloud-filled sky.

    There is the land
    green and rising
    and there is the heart
    empty of longing,
    with room at last
    for silence.

# Full of Grace

With open heart
morning floods in,
smoke-filled,
alive with birds.

Some ragged memory
with a broken muffler
pulls to the curb
but I wave it off.

What could be
more important
than the grove of silence?
All I need is there,
waiting, full of grace.

Drop the Skin Face

# Time to Live

Smoke rises from a chimney
into the cold December sky.
Desire, too, lifts above the earth
like a towering evergreen,
but the land calls from below:

discover yourself
wrapped in elk hide,
stone-faced and sober.

Stir the cauldron,
sing the ancient songs,
let the drumbeat of mother's heart
guide you in knowing
wild horse and flowing river.

You've died a thousand times;
now it's time to live.

## Grace to Her Becoming

Beneath the weight of snow
the Earth rests but does not sleep.

In root and caves beyond number
tribes of spring begin to drum,
waters destined for rivers flow,
and in the depths of her abundance
the burgeoning of new life.

Layer after layer the white blanket
covers Earth's repose, this peace
the grace to her becoming.

# Washboard Road

This rutted track
with potholes and cuts,
makes for rough travel.
Perhaps I should have
chosen a shorter course,
taken the highway.

Out on this spur
of lonely landscape
with wire fence
and barren fields,
two coyotes lope from cover;
a raptor watches.

Bouncing on the gravel
I wonder at my choices,
of wayward paths
and threadbare answers,
yet the hawk's eye catches me,
the coyotes' freedom
in their cold weather coats.

Keep going, I tell myself,
rolling open the window,
just over the next rise,
farther down the washboard road.

## Surrendered to Awakening

Two ravens appear
flying to the wooded point,
the sound of their bark
distinct from the call of crows.

Geese honk in vigilance,
then quiet as they take wing
toward a distant island.

Gulls cry plaintively,
winds sough through the trees,
dew lays sparkling upon the grass.

Deep mother of night
opens to father of day,
and I join the choir,
surrendered to awakening.

# Campground of His Ancient Home

Digging through the underbrush,
he cut his way through thorns
to the clean swath of river.
Guarded by boulders
and sheer stone walls,
the blue green water
flowed protected and fast.

Belly down on the gravel beach,
he drank from the river,
his thirst of many miles
defeating all ceremony.
In the far distance,
he heard Grandfather calling,
the sound of Grandmother's rattle.
He had come so far to see them,
to sit in their cornmeal circle
and know again the truth of his spirit.

A cool wind blew down the canyon
refreshing his washed face,
causing him to look up
to the distance he had yet to go.
All doubt was gone
for he could hear them calling,
and picking up his pack he set off,
ready to vault any barrier
for the campground of his ancient home.

# Soul Kitchen

Down I go once more
into the soul kitchen
where the dark soup
slowly cooks.

All the heartache
and worn-out beliefs
of the living and long gone
simmer over low flame
in the iron cauldron,
releasing the inedible
up the spirit flume,

melding what remains
by ancient recipe
into what will feed
until light returns.

## Janitor in the House of Soul

As janitor in the house of soul,
I work each night with broom and mop,
pushing an old cart through the dreamtime.
The body sleeps while I toil,
vacuuming worn books and shelves
filled with records of relationship.

There are lots of visitors
to inquire about family stories,
read the how-to books of salvation.
Not the librarian, only the janitor,
I dust the long tables and chairs
for those who do the night work.

You can spot the studious
with bent shoulders and bowed heads,
turning the yellowed pages of ancient tomes,
lips silently moving as they repeat incantations.

I keep to myself, one hand on the cart
and one on the beads I carry and thumb,
while I mop the tears and scrawl a few notes
of those I've loved and forgiven
before the lights go out in morning.

## An Old Tree Falls *(for Robert)*

He had gotten old
last time I saw him,
hair thinned white
though with fire in his belly.

He'd lit that flame for many,
bringing wildness
and passion
to the prisoners
of boredom.

We won't find
another like him
until we drop
into the dark pool
and recover the face
resting in deep water.

# Drop the Skin Face

I listen to the earth,
to the sound of the animal
that paws from within,
scratching at the door
for release into light.

How long it's taken,
the miles of dream track,
while the scent of morning
invited him out
for the pleasure of dirt.

I drop the skin face
and let the wolf loose,
his soft fur bristling
to roam and run free
in the sunlit forest
wet with desire.

Voicing the Incantation

# Rope of Stillness

I sit quite still,
becoming like the trees
in deep-rooted silence.

There is an old song
in the hushed music of the earth,
of ancient stone, rustling leaves
and forest dreaming.

I climb the vine-covered walls
using stillness as a braided rope,
and drop like a cat
into the garden of the eternal.

## Voicing the Incantation

Light returns as the earth slowly wakens.
Although warm in refuge, I feel the tug to rise
from beneath the woolen blanket.

The building creaks and groans
like my body in the first steps of morning.

A hymn of grace sounds within the earth,
melodies of joy and sorrow stirring,
to begin the journey from dark to light.

The old and broken seek repair,
and babes listen from the womb,
as elders finger their beads,

voicing the incantation of new life
aching to come forth.

# Rushing Tide

From caverns beneath the cold ground
ancient voices stir and ghost dancers
move their tireless feet
to the pulse of earth music.

Above and below urge us on,
to cross the waters of time,
toward the grail
that holds the lost truths
of our mysterious birth.

Into the rain we stumble
clawing on our oilskin jackets,
answering only to the sea
and the rock-bound shore
as we forge our way
into the rushing tide.

## Prepare for the Mountain

Looking within
I find seasoned wood
split and ready for the pyre.

I throw in with heretics
daring immolation,
snow monks melting ice
with silence.

The inner fire grows hot
as more of myself
turns into flame,
heat preparing me
for the distant mountain.

# Written Across the Sky

Light in the east
carves an opening
in the mass of clouds,
checking the rain with a sign
the storm may soon break.

We will yet suffer,
have to carry through
this dark night,
but in the end
the sun will rise
and we will find ourselves
in sight of the green land.

Noah will be there, and Moses,
Mary and her maidens
who treasured their oil
and kept a flame burning.
I will be there, looking for you,
remembering your face, your voice
and how you persevered.

Keep faith, my friend,
as I will in this struggle.
We have the promise
written across the sky,
foretelling the new earth
in all its bright-rimmed glory.

# Tear Another Page

There's light in the distance
where water shines,
though the island is buried
under gray clouds
beside a gunmetal sea.

Years past, the story goes,
we fell under the wings of a dark angel,
so long ago we can't remember
original color or the taste of freedom.

"You best be still and accept your fate,"
the elders told me, while by my eyes
they knew I wasn't a believer.
Most of them are dead and buried
while I keep dodging bullets.

Silently I move from word to word
to melt the bonds of the sleeping.
Awake in the greenwood,
I tear another page from the Book of Life
and feed it to the wind.

# Instead She Flowers *(for Mary)*

Autumn sweeps the laden trees,
spreading treasure on the ground
we cart off to a distant mill.

The soil aches for return
of what began in spring
and came to summer fullness.

You'd think the earth
would long ago surrender
but instead she flowers,

rising from her meager dirt
to fill the sky with color.

Where the River Goes

# For I Am Water

I hang on with aging roots,
the soil around me without comfort,
knowing my time may have passed,
and I a ghost left above ground.

Cautious of becoming bitter,
acidic to the green world,
I grow quiet, dissolved in silence.

Then like a branch lifted by the wind,
I understand my errors are the roots that hold me,
sorrow the knowing of the river,
how it rises and falls yet moves on.

I recall springs in the mountain cleft,
shining brown rocks where I stepped and fell,
the soft spread of green where creek joined river,
the mile-wide flow toward ocean sound.

There is no stopping, only the slow-bending curve,
the high bar of gravel; for I am water
and where the river goes, I go.

# Dark Green Solitude

Sun lights the valley;
along the coast a flood of rivers,
swollen bays, log-choked coves,
melting snow and full moon tides.

At rest in the quiet
without hunger or thirst,
the land teaches silence is enough
for a rivulet of dark green solitude
to nourish the earth.

# Where Bones Grind

The cherry trees
soaked in rain,
the valley skies
wrapped in gray.

I watch with faith
like a druid of old,
talking quietly
to the broken earth,
where bones grind,
and the lesson to go slow
takes form and speaks.

Patiently, I wait
with the cherry trees,
roots sunk beneath
the pavement,
drawing up beauty
from the soil
I've been given.

# In the Hour Before Dawn

Tell you what I'll do.
I'll scrub the world with steel wool,
scrape away the grimy bits
of cruelty and war,
put soap and water
to sorrow and despair.

Fresh flowers on all the graves,
remembrances for the forgotten.
Silence to cleanse the tangle of sound
then starlight for speaking.

When you awake, you'll find tears
of kindness watering the garden,
and green earth waiting.
That's what I'll do
for you this morning.

# Before the Sky Grows Dark

Massive white clouds
bank against the mountains
while a blue gray blanket

spreads over the sea.
Nootka roses bloom
as the camas wilt and fade.

The chitter of birds in the forest,
the cry of gulls across the bay
and the slow beating of my heart.

Is that enough to draw you near
before the sky grows dark
and night closes in?

# Choirs of Knowing

Rain clouds pass
and Orion appears in the eastern sky,
the first signal cold is near.

I walk out on the wind-whipped point
to relish the bright lamp of Jupiter,
the glowing red of Mars and the array
of stars in the vast spread of cosmos.

As one voice from the silent planet,
I send greetings to the star nation,
to all my kin in the realm of the Maker.

Somehow, across impossible distance,
their signals reach back, tremulous
and shining with songs of the light bearers,
choirs of knowing in the deep dark of night.

# Words of the Disciple

The tangle of roots in mud and clay
hold the impossible height
swaying above the rooftops.

I burrow down in what's left
of imagination, clawing through
wires and pipes to the soil past grief,
finding a grip in the broken clods
to recall your face, your name,
the years when strength was real.

I fought the greater force and lost
though you'd never tell by the smile
I wear like a medal of honor
from the wars of insanity.

Grace can be forgotten,
but the slender threads
of love's splendid garment,
torn and spoiled with mud,
will not be undone.

With arthritic hands
I reach out in morning light,
caress the dawn as it lifts the sky.

Scatter my ashes below the evergreen,
let me be food for the gnarl of roots,
and from the darkest earth let me rise,
let me rise.

# Dark Heaven

Morning under clouded skies,
the longest night passed
in the slow turn
toward brighter days.

Aldebaran leads Orion
through the winter arc
as I pursue the star within
on the road leading home.

Be of good faith, my friend;
though we have far to travel,
we are connected, however distant,
following a light in the dark heaven.

# Then We Will Not Speak

After the storms pass
and the hungry ones
are driven from their feed,
the humble will wait
in the calm sloughs
of spring beauty.

There you will find me
sore-boned and broken,
returned from the
battlefields of poetry.

Then we will not speak
nor write a single word
for on that surging tide
silence will prevail.

# About the Author

Author of four volumes of poetry, Slender Arrow (1998), Out From Under (2001), The Living Dark (2006), The Irish Girl (2017), Don publishes the online weekly Poet's Journal. He attended college at the University of Notre Dame where he has returned several times as a guest speaker in language arts.

He had an extensive career in construction project management, including major facilities for many non-profits throughout the Pacific Northwest. With his wife, artist and glass sculptor Linda Ethier, he lives between the San Juan Islands of Washington and Portland Oregon.

Don Hynes

www.ingramcontent.com/pod-product-compliance
Lightning Source LLC
Chambersburg PA
CBHW032040290426
44110CB00012B/880